Coping

turning pain into blessing

Mostyn Roberts

EP BOOKS

Registered Office: 140 Coniscliffe Road, Darlington, Co. Durham, UK DL3 7RT

www.epbooks.org
admin@epbooks.org

EP Books are distributed in the USA by:

www.jplbooks.com
orders@jplbooks.com

and

100fThose Ltd
www.100fthose.com
sales.us@100fthose.com

British Library Cataloguing in Publication Data available

Print ISBN 978-1-78397-301-9

Contents

Introduction

A pastor, surely, should be able to take criticism. After all, criticism is only words, and while sticks and stones may break your bones, words will never hurt you.

That is the theory. Some criticism does wash off the backs of most of us making little impact, but much of it hurts. Some of it can be debilitating, sapping joy in your work, confidence in the exercise of your gifts and even assurance of your call to ministry. It has the potential to destroy a ministry and do deep and lasting damage to a church.

You will not have been a minister long before experiencing it and of course you may well deserve it—perhaps more than you actually get if you have a charitable church and fellow church officers. By no means all criticism of a pastor is unjustified or malicious, and the last thing I want to do is to give the impression that a minister is above criticism or should retire into a shell of pious self-pity or adopt the 'how dare you, I am the pastor' stance the moment he receives it.

There is another side of the coin, too familiar to some Christians, where churches suffer from heavy handed or bullying pastors. Any hint of disagreement is swiftly, and sometimes bruisingly, dismissed or squashed. Pastors must always be ready to examine their hearts to see if this describes them. In not dealing with such situations here I am not suggesting they are unimportant; they are simply beyond my present aim.

I do, however, want to try to offer help to pastors who are being, or may be, wounded by criticism. The aim is not so much to offer sympathy as to enable the pastor who is under the lash to face it biblically, that is to turn the experience of criticism into something useful and fruitful to God, for yourself and for the church.

This booklet began life as a paper given at a local fraternal (ministers' meeting). I am grateful to those fellow ministers who meet at Welwyn not only for their friendship over many years, but for their thoughtful reception of that presentation. That response and my own sense that this is something that could be useful for ministers more widely, has led me to offer it as a source of help to pastors and other church leaders facing criticism and sometimes worse in their churches.

Although any Christian might find help here, the book is evidently written with church leaders in mind. I use the titles 'pastor' and 'minister' interchangeably—but you'll know who you are!

I should like to thank the members of my

present church, Welwyn Evangelical, for all their encouragement to me over the years.

Mostyn Roberts

What Jesus and Paul faced

In a former church at a difficult time an old lady gave me a cutting from a magazine headed 'It's not personal!' When a soldier is in the trenches, said this little article addressed to ministers facing criticism, what does he expect? He does not object to every bullet that flies over his head saying 'why are you getting at me?' He is there to fight. It is a battle. He has the uniform on. Of course he is going to get shot at. It's stupid to take it personally.

That doesn't tell the whole story, but it helped at the time, and there is a good measure of truth in it. It also helped to know that an old saint saw things like that and was thinking of me and no doubt praying for me. It reminded me that as a pastor, I will get criticised; it comes with the territory.

Of course ministers frequently deserve criticism, often more than they get, so charitable are many of the Lord's people. Their own attitudes are often the biggest problem in coping with it. Pride is a big issue for many ministers, and that leads to self-righteousness, defensiveness and self-pity in adversity. Remember too that leadership in all contexts attracts criticism—think of the way we criticise our politicians, chief executives and football managers. It comes with the turf. You take the blame, sometimes fairly, sometimes not, when things are going wrong.

Yet for the pastor there is more to it than this. He is a man of God, a servant of Jesus Christ. To try to understand the criticism that even a good and godly pastor receives, therefore, we begin with the experience of our Lord and Master.

The Experience of Jesus

Jesus faced conflict of many kinds. Although there were times of popularity and acclaim, Jesus' life was marked by conflict which finally came to a head at the cross. He warned his disciples that the servant is not above the master and that if the world hated him they should expect it to hate them (Matthew 10:24, John 15:18). Jesus warns his disciples he is sending them out as sheep among wolves (Matthew 10:16f). The pastor will soon learn that wolves can wear sheep's clothing, that some get into the sheepfold and that even sheep have a nasty bite.

It is instructive to see the reasons for opposition to Jesus. Opposition is a wider category than criticism but I think we can see in the kind of opposition that the Lord faced the roots of many of the criticisms we face. Opposition to and criticism of Jesus were of course always unjustified. Much that we receive will to some extent be justified. Criticism of Jesus was always ultimately diabolical, arising from unbelief and hatred of God. Much that we receive will be constructive; all of it will be God's fatherly chastisement of us.

I have drawn the following instances of Jesus facing opposition from the gospels of Matthew and John.

Jesus was criticised for being who he was in a world that did not recognize him. More than once Jesus was accused of blasphemy—for forgiving sins (Matthew 9:3); or 'making himself equal with God' (John 5:18; 10:29–33). The irony was of course that Jesus was God but his opponents did not recognise it. He was simply being himself, acting out of his true nature.

As a minister you will experience something of this. You are not the Lord Jesus, but you are a servant of God in a position of immense privilege and importance. Your very existence as a man of God doing your duty will attract opposition. People who oppose you may not realise what it is that causes their antagonism; there will often be a 'without a cause' element to criticism you receive (John 15:25). It will be rationalised in all sorts of ways, but don't be surprised when opponents cannot give a clear, and certainly not a satisfactory, reason for their criticisms. You represent him whom the world hates and whose Son it put to death. You cannot expect anything else.

Jesus was repeatedly misunderstood and it

is instructive to consider the people—often surprising—who could not grasp what he was about. He was misunderstood by John the Baptist, who had believed in him and prepared the way for his coming (Matthew 11:1-3). 'Are you really the Messiah?' John had asked. Jesus was not matching up to expectations. Do you know the feeling of people questioning your call, competence or credentials? Perhaps it is someone who has been your friend, someone who really does love you but … well, you are disappointing them, disappointing the people, not meeting expectations.

Jesus was misunderstood by his family—his mother and brothers did not understand him (Matthew 12:46-50). His mother was a believer, his brothers at this stage were not, and so the agenda that drove Jesus' life was opaque to the brothers, perhaps a little more clear to Mary. Jesus made the point that those who did his Father's will were his true family. As a minister you will sometimes feel that few understand you, and that those few are not necessarily those humanly nearest to you.

Jesus was misunderstood by his closest disciple, Peter (Matthew 16:22-23). There was no doubt about Peter's devotion to the Lord, nor about his genuine faith. He had a way to go of course, both down (his denial) and up (his leadership in the early church). Yet at Caesarea Philippi he became Satan's mouthpiece. The Father had revealed to Peter that Jesus is 'the Christ, the Son of the living God' (Matthew 16:16), but Peter immediately betrayed his lack of understanding of what that means. His thinking was still that of the world and even of Satan.

Satan had failed in his direct attempt to derail Jesus at the outset of his ministry, but he now succeeded in getting his voice heard by the Son of God. How? Through the Lord's chief disciple. What a coup for the Evil One! We have to listen, weigh and sift what we hear, even from those closest to us—even from those who genuinely believe, and who love us. Misunderstanding, opposition and even satanic temptation from those closest to them will be familiar to many pastors.

Jesus was the victim of fickleness. He compared his generation to children sitting in the market place calling to their playmates (Matthew 11:16–19). They criticised John the Baptist because he was ascetic; they criticised Jesus because he ate and drank normally. Some people are hard to please; some are never satisfied. Sadly the criticism sometimes levelled at pastors is no more mature or discerning than that of fickle children. You just haven't pleased them. Be discerning about such criticism. You can't ignore it, but you must take notice of it because of what it tells you about the spiritual state of the flock more than what it says about you.

Most of Jesus' opposition came from the religious

hierarchy (Matthew 6:3f; chapters 21–27). There were vested interests and fear of loss of prestige, position and power; they recognized that the parable of the talents was told against them (Matthew 21:33–46). Jesus portrayed them as opposing God's purposes for themselves and his people. He challenged the religious establishment and they hated him (cf. John 7:7; 11:53) and his followers, even putting them out of the synagogue (John 9:13–22) and killing them (John 12:10–11).

You are in the front line of a clash of kingdoms. Jesus' kingdom is not of this world (John 18:36) and you represent that kingdom. As my opening illustration reminds us, you are in a battle; what do you expect? You represent Truth in a world governed by the Lie (John 18:37–38; cf Romans 1:25). Jesus is the Truth, speaks the truth and bears witness to the truth. 'Have I then become your enemy by telling you the truth?' asks Paul of the wayward Galatians (Galatians 4:16). Well, yes, that can be the pastor's experience, you do become the enemy of some. Don't be surprised by opposition to the truth. The only safe ground is the Word of God which is truth (John 17:17).

Jesus' authority was challenged (Matthew 21:23–27), again principally by the chief priests and elders. Some people dislike authority. There are such people in our churches, who pay lip service to submission to authority but in practice it means they submit when they like what those in authority are doing. This is not what the Bible has in mind when it tells us to obey our leaders and submit to them (Hebrew 13:17). If authority is valid, it is to be obeyed precisely when we do not like what it is telling us; otherwise we, and not the one vested with it, are the final authority.

Your authority as a minister is of course not in yourself. It is first of all in the Word of God, and must always be exercised whether in teaching, pastoral care or church discipline, in subjection to the Word. But it is also in your office. There is authority in the office of eldership. It is to be exercised in the service of the church, but it is still authority. There will sadly always be a dislike of such authority among some Christians. Immature Christians 'hate discipline' (Psalm 50:17). The cultural dislike of authority so prevalent today is only the latest manifestation of this very human (and satanic) disposition. The fifth commandment condemns many who like to apply it to their children but not to themselves.

Resistance to authority will cause you grief; there is a danger that you may be provoked to react to such opposition. You may become authoritarian, imposing your will on the church and justify it by grumbling: 'People don't respect authority any more!' Alternatively you may back off and abandon any exercise of true authority. The right exercise

of authority in servant leadership is never easy,
but do not let criticism make you react in either a
cowardly way or a bullying way.

Jesus pointed out the world's hatred of him and
those he sends in his name (John 7:7; 15:18). This
is irrational—'without a cause' (15:25, citing Psalm
35:19). The emphasis is again on the inevitability
of opposition to those walking in the master's
footsteps. It often cannot be reasoned with. The
people who hate you do not necessarily know
why they do. Discussion can sometimes get to the
bottom of an issue, but not always. The world's
hatred of God after all is utterly irrational; the
pastor will 'cop' some of it.

Jesus was criticized for what he did, for example
breaking religious traditions, especially those
surrounding the sabbath (Matthew 12:1-14; John
5:16; 9:13-16). In addition he broke with cultural
and social taboos, for example when he spoke with
Samaritan woman at the well (John 4:27) and when
he deliberately ate with those designated 'sinners'
(Matthew 9:11; 15:1-20). Jesus, unlike us, never
broke the law of God, but his radical obedience cut
through many pharisaic and cultural impositions.
Obedience to God often does.

The faithful servant of God will have to challenge
things that some Christians have held dear for
years. The reformed church should always be
reforming, and an important part of your ministry

is to try to bring the people of God under the actual (as opposed to the merely theoretical) direction of Scripture. People will often *listen to* teaching that they do not like; what provokes anger is when you try to *do* something. Changing the way a church worships, for example, has been a familiar field of battle in recent years. Some changes by ministers admittedly make one wish congregations had protested more. Nonetheless churches can be tenacious in holding on to practices both traditional and 'contemporary' in many areas of church life, that need patient teaching and careful application to change.

You will suffer for such challenges. 'Avoid unnecessary offence' is good advice, but some offences are necessary. Try to avoid giving offence, other than the necessary offence of the gospel, but people will *take* offence when you are simply doing your duty.

We see the outworking in history of the battle in the spiritual realms portrayed in Revelation 12, where the dragon having missed his opportunity to destroy the heavenly child, now takes out his anger on the church. You as a pastor are in the front line of that battle. Do not be surprised at the fiery trial that comes upon you.

Jesus suffered from people's unbelief and spiritual blindness. The unbeliever is spiritually blind and too often is led, in religion, by 'blind guides' (Matthew

15:14). The Pharisees accused Jesus of being empowered by Beelzebul (Matthew 12:24); their sin in that case, said Jesus, was unforgivable. The human heart is evil (Matthew 12:34). If you go about doing good as Jesus did (Acts 10:38) you will suffer.

Unbelief is ultimately behind all of the opposition Jesus endured. Unbelief does not understand who Jesus is; it does not understand why he came; it does not see its own need; it is in continual rebellion against God, his works and his servants. It will not have God's Son rule over it and is prepared to murder him to protect its autonomy.

You may wonder what this has to do with the church; after all, are we not all believers? Well, there will be unbelief in the visible church. Sometimes those who even the church officers trust are saved will in fact be unconverted.

A symptom of unbelief is that it looks for a sign—a sign from heaven, in Jesus' case something really spectacular that would 'prove' to the people of his day that he was truly a prophet or the Messiah (Matthew 12:38–39; 16:1–4). These demands by the Pharisees were in spite of the miracles Jesus had actually performed.

'Prove yourself—on our terms' is the demand of some. The requirement is to match up to their standards. Maybe your preaching is not what they would like; or is not up to the standard of your predecessor; or of the popular and thriving church a few miles away; and certainly not up to their favourite preacher on the internet. Perhaps the church is not growing; you are not adopting the 'successful' methods of another church they have read about. Even a ministry where much is happening will not be immune to criticism if people judge the minister by their own criteria.

What is the real motivation when a godly minister faces the demand to prove himself? It is a refusal to walk by faith. The minister—assuming he is really called and has been legitimately appointed by the church—is now asked to establish his credentials according to unbiblical standards. Ministers are not above accountability, but let the standards by which you are judged be biblical ones. Don't allow the pharisaic, unbelieving demand for signs to crush you.

There will also be weak faith in believers. Some will be making slow (if any) progress in sanctification; even the more mature will have blind spots. You will also be distressed by the weakness of faith in your own heart. Jesus had to rebuke his disciples for their little faith (Matthew 8:26). Criticism will be one of the manifestations of weak faith: Jesus was criticised for being asleep in the storm: 'Master, do you not care that we are perishing?' (Mark 4:38). The church is in trouble and nothing is being done. The leadership appears to be asleep. It maybe the leadership *is* asleep and so such comments should not be automatically dismissed. But bear in mind that such criticism could be the symptom of weak faith—people forget that storms will come, that Satan is hostile and the Lord is always awake to the plight of his people.

Jesus was denied by a true but weak disciple (Matthew 26:30-35, 69-75). Peter, despite his brave protestations, was intimidated by the situation in the high priest's courtyard. There are plenty of good people who fail at vital moments, perhaps under intense pressure—perhaps you have been one of them. Or perhaps you have relied on people in a difficult time, or in a controversial issue and found that they suddenly back down. Fear is often the motive, of friends or family and the result is that you are left isolated, exposed. The person who has let you down may certainly be a true believer and they may be terribly sorry, but they are weak. You are hurt, the church is damaged. What do you do? You know how Jesus treated Peter: he forgave and in due time restored him. That must be our model. It may not always work out but even in the worst case there may be repentance and that must result in restoration, as in Peter's case.

Jesus' teaching provoked grumbling—for example when many of his followers left him at Capernaum because of his 'hard sayings' (John 6:41, 60-61, 66). There will always be people who do not like the straight teaching of the Word of God. Three or four people once walked out of a sermon on Acts when my exposition challenged their firm belief that we are still living in the apostolic age and should expect apostolic miracles today. Of course I was not denying the possibility of miracles altogether. On another occasion a couple, who were not members but had been attending regularly, stopped coming because they did not like the insistence on effort in the Christian life. They wanted constant affirmations of grace without obligation.

Sometimes people's objections will be because of firmly held principles; at other times it will be because your teaching is irksome to the flesh. John's gospel is peppered with occasions where people misunderstand Jesus' teaching, from the Jews' misunderstanding his saying about rebuilding the temple (2:20) to Nicodemus' crass misunderstanding of the new birth (3:4) and the crowd's misunderstanding about the bread of life (6:41, 60–61, 66).

Jesus knew how to distinguish believing ignorance from hostile muttering. With his disciples he was patient to explain (Mark 8:14–21); other grumbling he knew was due to unbelief, the fruit of the flesh, not the Spirit (John 6:63–64). Moses had to endure repeated grumbling from the Israelites about lack of water or bread, or the hardship of the way, even to the point of wishing they had never left Egypt (Exodus 15:24, 16:2–3; 17:2–7; Numbers 11:1–4; 16:12–14; 20:3; 21:5). God made it clear they were really grumbling against him (Exodus 16:7–8; Numbers 14:26–27). It was in the end symptomatic of unbelief that refused to believe God and enter the Promised Land. The pastor will sometimes bear the brunt of criticism from people who are simply discontented, disappointed, ungrateful and unhappy with God's dealings with them. Sometimes this will be the fruit of sheer unbelief.

Confusion about Jesus was evident in his day, as at the Feast of Tabernacles related in John chapter 7. His brothers revealed their unbelief (vv.3–5). The crowds were divided about him—some said the Lord was a good man, others that he was leading people astray (v.12). They knew he came from Galilee but that meant he could not be the Christ; others thought he was (v.41). They were in a muddle. Unbelief was of course widespread (12:37–50) as was hatred, even after recent popular acclaim (Matthew 27:19–24).

People are often muddled. They are sheep, to be loved, but they need a shepherd and the shepherd is to lead, not follow. Central to pastoral leadership is teaching. You must preach the whole counsel of God and sometimes it will provoke a hostile reaction. That may be from the unbeliever who does not believe he needs to repent or is a sinner.

Hostility may sometimes be from Christians. At times you will be aware that your message is likely to touch a raw spot; a minister told me that the most adverse reaction to any sermons he had preached was to a series on corporate worship. At other times the hostile reaction will take you completely unawares; you will just have touched a raw nerve.

Respond wisely and try to distinguish at least between believing ignorance and hostile muttering. Show the wisdom that is open to reason (James 3:17). Let your 'gentle reasonableness' be known to all (Philippians 4:5, my translation). Directly after a service you will often be vulnerable and may react heatedly to criticism, so you need to be especially aware of that danger at such a time.

A minister wants to encourage the Berean spirit—searching the Scriptures to see if these things are so (Acts 17:11). Doing more to help congregations assess the content of sermons intelligently is probably something we could all do better. But here we are talking about the negative reaction which, unlike the diligent Bereans, does not receive the word with all eagerness. What kind of issue is it? It could be doctrinal but is it more or less an intellectual disagreement, or is the belief particularly precious to that person in which case the emotions are more involved? Certain issues are precious to some people out of all proportion to their importance—one thinks of the priority some Christians attach to views of the millennium. It is more important to them than (dare I suggest?) its place in the biblical scheme of things demands. Their problem may not be doctrinal at all and you have just touched on something that triggered an emotional reaction. I noticed once that a member of the congregation who had been coming fairly regularly for a while, suddenly stopped talking to me though he kept coming to church. I learned some time later that it was because something I had said had smitten the conscience of a woman with whom he was having a relationship and she called a halt to it. The man blamed me, convinced that I had deliberately torpedoed the relationship.

You can never predict (thankfully) what the preaching of the Word will do, but you can be sure that if it is faithful, at some time or another it will provoke opposition and criticism.

There was of course *outright opposition to Jesus* and some ministers will experience that. Religious leaders plotted against the Lord (Matthew 22:15). Few experiences are more demoralizing for a pastor than to realize that church members, and sometimes his fellow leaders, are plotting against him. It is utterly undermining, one of the loneliest situations any minister could ever face. Everything, apart from your family, that means most to you— your life's work, your calling, your people—is being taken from you. It is a bereavement. Such situations send the pastor to his knees. Then you realize in the Lord's presence that, of course, they are not your people, they are his, and he is looking after them, but that nonetheless you have a duty to fight wolves and not run away like a hired hand. Sometimes the moment of becoming aware of such orchestrated opposition is the most painful part of the experience; once you realize you are in a fight and steel up for it, things become, in a way, easier.

Jesus was challenged by scoffing unbelievers. The Sadducees asked Jesus about the wife married successively to seven brothers—whose wife would she be in the resurrection? They did not believe in the resurrection and wanted to ridicule it (Matthew 22:23–33). Note how seriously Jesus answers them, using even maliciously motivated questions for teaching. Cynics like this are usually less difficult to deal with than people who profess to believe yet oppose you. At least you know where you are with them.

The Lord was questioned by biased testers wanting him to fail. The Pharisees, more conventional in their theology than the Sadducees, questioned him on their favourite subject, the law (Matthew 22:34–40). Their opposition was slightly different from the Sadducees, perhaps less cynical. Some may be brought to faith, as Jesus indicates when one answered him wisely: 'You are not far from the kingdom of God' affirms the Lord (Mark 12:32–34). Jesus gave his opponents straight answers, regardless of their motives, and sometimes the result was sympathy.

Envy will motivate some. Pilate saw that this was behind the religious leaders' attack on Jesus (Matthew 27:18). They hated the threat he posed to their power and prestige. Some people will be very conscious of your position and status, as they see it, and want to put you in your place, even humiliate you. Moses experienced this. His brother Aaron and sister Miriam criticised him for marrying a Cushite woman but phrased their complaint in terms suggesting resentment of his status: 'Has the Lord indeed spoken only through Moses? Has he not spoken through us also?' (Numbers 12:2). Korah, Moses' cousin, a Levite, later led a rebellion against Moses and Aaron, taking the moral high ground of egalitarianism: "You have gone too far! For all in the congregation are holy, every one of them, and the Lord is among them. Why then do you exalt yourselves above the assembly of the Lord?' (Numbers 16:3). Moses made it very clear that it was envy that motivated the rebels: not content with being Levites they wanted to be priests. It was they, not Moses, who had 'gone too far' (16:7–10).

Jesus was betrayed by Judas, a disciple, though it was something Jesus had known would happen all along (John 6:70). Few experiences are more painful than to be betrayed by a friend. These are not always false brethren, like Judas the 'son of destruction' (John 17:12) but some may be. Judas' motives included money (Matthew 26:14–16) but Scripture reveals a darker spiritual background—Satan had entered him (John 13:27).

Some people just get carried along with a hostile tide; they are under pressure from family and friends and you may have disappointed them, annoyed them or crossed them in some way. Fairness to you takes second place to their loyalty to their friends or perhaps as they see it, the church. Did Judas, like the Pharisees, see Jesus as threatening everything he held dear and that gave him security? You suddenly realize you are being stabbed in the back. It is bitterly painful, but you will not be the first or the last to have gone through it.

Opposition, including criticism, can be brutal. Brutality in Jesus' case was physical (Matthew 27:27–31), and many pastors and other Christians in the history of the church and today know only too well what that means. In the modern West physical brutality may be rare but the verbal and emotional harshness of some so-called Christians can be incredible. Some pastors know what it is to sit in a church meeting and have to listen to criticism and humiliation poured upon them that would be considered unacceptable amongst non-Christians.

The Lord also faced mockery (Matthew 27:27–44). The soldiers mocked his kingship; the crowds derided what they understood to be his claim to destroy and rebuild the temple; they scoffed at the idea that he was the Son of God; chief priests, scribes and elders scorned the idea that he could save others if he could not save himself.

These experiences may not be familiar to you personally, but mockery can come in different forms, often subtle, even genteel. It may be suggested that you are too old or too young; perhaps the suggestion is that you are too conventional, too traditional or too trendy. People will describe you as overly dogmatic or insufficiently decisive—it is not unusual to hear two conflicting criticisms on the same day! Paul warned Timothy 'Let no-one despise your youth' (1 Timothy 4:12): perhaps if he were writing today he would warn about despising older brothers! The most serious aspect of mockery is that people are simply finding one reason or another for not listening to you: 'What, you believe that?' As a result the label 'fundamentalist' or some other term intended to be derogatory is applied. You have been put in a category, a box, and whether it is related to age, doctrine, personality or style, that box says 'Not to be listened to with any seriousness.'

Jesus was criticized by all kinds of people. It is worthwhile reminding ourselves of the diverse sources of the criticism the Lord received. The list is instructive and sobering: a friend, John the Baptist, through misunderstanding the nature of the Messiah's ministry; his family, through at best misunderstanding, but also unbelief; a loving disciple, Peter, also through misunderstanding the Messiah's ministry, thinking 'as men think' and allowing himself to be used as Satan's mouthpiece; a false disciple (Judas) through the influence of Satan, malice and greed; the religious powers through fear of losing power and prestige (and no doubt, in their opinion, a genuine concern for their religion); the public through ignorance, confusion, being easily led; the state, in its weakness and expediency.

Behind it all is a spiritual hatred inspired by Satan who is specifically mentioned as influencing the Pharisees and other leaders, possessing Judas and getting his voice heard even in the place closest to Jesus, through Peter.

God's sovereignty

Now for some good news. It is abundantly clear that behind all the opposition Jesus faced was the will of God, as he indicated when he prophesied his own sufferings and death. There was a divine *must* in his life (Matthew 16:21). Judas' betrayal is prophesied in the psalms (John 13:18, Psalm 41:9); John reminds us that Jesus' sufferings fulfil Scripture (John 19:24,36; cf. Acts 4:28).

There is of course a whole biblical theology of God's sovereignty behind this. Can something as unpleasant as the criticism and hostile, even malicious, opposition I am facing truly be the will of God for me? Yet the Scriptures remind us: 'Is it not from the mouth of the Most High that good and bad come?' (Lamentations 3:38); 'I make well-being and create calamity' (Isaiah 45:7); 'As for you, you meant it for evil against me, but God meant it for good ...' (Genesis 50:20). The cross, planned in the eternal purpose of God yet executed in history by wicked men (Acts 2:23), shows his all-embracing sovereignty over all things, *for good*. Even that nastiness you are facing at present cannot come from any source outside the providential will of God, nor find its ultimate purpose anywhere beyond his good purposes for you and his church. There is *nowhere* outside that will or those purposes.

One of the most encouraging truths in my own experience has been that 'the Lamb is on the throne.' I was driving home one wintry evening from a supermarket in the town where I was then a minister and things were at their most difficult in the church. I was listening to a sermon on Revelation 5. The preacher emphasized that truth: 'the Lamb is on the throne.' It struck deep into my heart, and gave me not only encouragement, but great joy. I know of no more delightful truth for the pastor or any Christian than that of God's sovereignty, which is always allied of course with his goodness and, for his people, with his grace. All things do work together for good for those who are called according to his purpose, and they do so not simply because God is running along after the event picking up the pieces, but because he has decreed all things in the first place. We run a race marked out for us (Hebrews 12:1).

The third verse of William Cowper's hymn *God moves in a mysterious way* has often been a help to me:

> You fearful saints, fresh courage take
> The clouds you so much dread
> Are big with mercy, and shall break
> In blessings on your head.

The Experience of Paul

Paul was perhaps the greatest servant of the Lord Jesus Christ in the history of the church, but he experienced a great deal of opposition from within churches. In the New Testament, most of this appears to have come from the churches in Corinth and Galatia.

In Corinth the root was worldliness in the church—a worldly standard for leadership and unfavourable comparison of Paul with others. This showed itself in different ways. There were divisions and personality cults in the church (1 Corinthians 1:12;

3:1–9:) showing a tendency to glory in men rather than the Lord.

Worldliness shows itself in both flattery and criticism. Many ministers would say that spiritually the former is more dangerous than the latter. Some people will love to put you on a pedestal. In the first place this is an unspiritual attitude, and such people can as easily and very quickly turn against you. Some ministers find that their harshest critics over the years are those who were warmest in their welcome early on. Secondly, flattery is divisive because if they are for you, the likelihood is they are against someone else. If that attitude is allowed to grow in a church, there will be parties and factions in no time—and you will suffer along with everyone else.

Paul was not meeting the Corinthians' expectations (1 Corinthians 4:10–13). They thought he really was not sophisticated enough for them. Many pastors will know that feeling. His credentials were attacked—he did not claim his rights as any decent teacher would do (2 Corinthians 11:9; 12:13; 1 Corinthians 9:1–18). The specific issues will not be the same today, but pastors will often be criticised for not being good enough for one reason or another. The truth of course is that we are not good enough and we know it; who is sufficient for these things (2 Corinthians 2:16)? Our answer is that our sufficiency is in Christ (2 Corinthians 3:5-6). The Corinthian attack was wrongly directed: Paul never did claim to be sufficient in worldly terms, nor is any minister. People who attack you on worldly grounds can be very hurtful, but in the end your authority is not based upon such criteria but on God's call on your life.

Paul was particularly criticised for his weak presence and speech (2 Corinthians 10:8-10; 11:6). Many of us, I am sure, know what it is to have our preaching criticised and much of it will be only too justified. Any minister wants to improve in this, as in every area. But the problem again in Corinth was the worldly criteria of assessment. We must be very careful to apply only biblical criteria to our preaching, not the world's idea of what makes a great speaker.

Paul was, finally, unfairly accused of being vacillating when he was really making necessary changes for the sake of the Corinthians. Such criticism arose out of misunderstanding, but also a readiness to impute false motives based on an underlying hostility (2 Corinthians 1:17f.). It is sad when people are too quick to impute bad faith to a minister—it reveals a lack of trust and of grace.

The problem in Galatia was false teaching and immature Christians. Paul was opposed by preachers of a different gospel and those influenced by them. It was an issue of fundamental importance, an attack on the gospel of justification by grace through faith alone (Galatians 1:6-9; 4:8-9). The false teachers were 'troubling' the Galatians (5:10, 12). Had he become their enemy by telling them the truth (4:16)? His opponents flattered the Galatians, causing them to desert Paul (4:17, 6:12-13).

Obviously immaturity will always be present in the church and we ourselves may sometimes find we are guilty of it. The false teaching that troubled the Galatian churches can seem more remote, but the influence of some television and internet preachers and books from undiscerning bookshops can have a similar effect. Unwary Christians may find themselves absorbing false teaching.

The pastor has a duty to stand up firmly for the truth and will sometimes find himself having to name false teachings and those who spread them. We do not want a negative ministry that cultivates popularity by naming and attacking others, but there are times when it is necessary to publicly expose and oppose false teaching. Paul had to rebuke Peter in to prevent false teaching (Galatians 2:11-14). The letter to the Galatians shows clearly the pain a pastor can feel when his flock is hijacked by false teachers (1:6; 3:1; 4:12-20; 5:7-12).

Responding to Criticism:
Jesus and Paul

How did Jesus respond?

The general picture is that Jesus persevered in doing good. He set his face like flint (Isaiah 50:7); he set his face to go to Jerusalem (Luke 9:51). His meat was to do the will of his Father, the one who had sent him (John 4:34). He would not be diverted.

What is striking is how often the 'doing good' turns out to be teaching. There was no greater good the Lord could do than to teach the word, the word of truth, the word of eternal life. Though it was often just that word that attracted the criticism and opposition, his response to criticism was to teach some more.

More specifically, when he was criticized for 'being who he was' he simply used the occasion to teach his opponents and others and pressed on (Matthew 9:4-6). When misunderstood, he again taught—for example after John the Baptist doubted his identity (Matthew 11:4-19); or when his family wanted to 'speak to him' (12:46-50). When he detected Satanic opposition he was blunt, as with Peter (16:23), but he went on to teach (16:24-28).

He taught when people were fickle (11:16-19). He was not afraid to point out how childish his critics in this instance were. His harshest words were always for the hostile religious leaders. Whether they opposed him for challenging their traditions (12:11-14, 15:1-20) or displayed spiritual blindness (15:14), unbelief (12:38, 16:1) or doubt as to his authority (21:23f), Christ was not afraid to be blunt. Yet he taught (12:39-42; 16:1-4; 21:28f) and he wanted even them to be saved. As the father of the two sons in the parable would have welcomed the elder son to come to the feast (Luke 15:31-32) Jesus pleaded with the Pharisees, 'even if you do not believe me, believe the works, that you may know and understand that the Father is in me and I am in the Father' (John 10:38). He did not shut them out of the kingdom; they excluded themselves.

When betrayed he saw the hand of both divine purpose and Satanic opposition and let judgement take its course (John 6:70, 17:12, 13:27). When denied, he was gracious with the weak disciple and provided for his restoration (Matthew 26:30-35, John 21:15-19). In suffering brutality and mockery he prayed for the forgiveness of those who did not know what they were doing (Luke 23:34).

Although in general he was compassionate with the crowds, Jesus was direct with people when need be and even sounded harsh, but when was this? First, when people needed to know the cost of salvation. You cannot promise to follow Jesus without counting the cost, without realising that the life of the kingdom is prior to natural ties, and without putting him ahead of all other claims (Luke 9:57-62). Second, when their faith was likely to be superficial. People may follow even Jesus from carnal motives (John 6:26) or without realising the radical nature of his claims (John 8:31-38). Third, and most markedly, when, as in the case of the Pharisees and other religious leaders, they misled the people and opposed his mission. He attacked the false teachings of the scribes and Pharisees and did not spare the false teachers themselves—vipers, wolves, hypocrites. But this was not out of revenge or vindictiveness. The 'woes' he pronounces (23:1-36) are not expressions of personal hurt, pique or vengeance; they are a divine curse on false prophets and a reproof of false teaching. In all things Jesus went about doing good (Acts 10:38), preaching the message of the kingdom, knowing what his end would be. A lesson to be seen in and learned from the life of Moses is his intercession for the people who repeatedly grumbled and complained against him (Number 12:13; 14:13; 16:22,41-48; 21:7) while he also called for justice to be executed on flagrant offenders (Exodus 32:26; Numbers 16:16f). A merciful spirit and the application of discipline are not mutually exclusive.

Jesus knew that all he endured was in his father's hands and that what he was experiencing was ordained for him. 'When he was reviled he did not revile in return; when he suffered, he did not threaten, but continued entrusting himself to him who judges justly' (1 Peter 2:23). He knew that in the end God would be victorious.

How did Paul respond?

Note how much Paul, like his Lord, uses occasions of opposition and criticism as platforms for teaching.

Pre-eminent is his conviction of his call (1 Corinthians 4:19–20; 2 Corinthians 1:23). Paul knows not only that God has saved him but commissioned him to be an apostle. Every one of his letters contains an assertion in some form of his being a servant of Christ Jesus. Am I really called? That question will cross the mind of every conscientious minister when he is under attack. By 'call' I am not talking about a major experiential crisis or a 'voice from heaven', but the inner conviction, however you may have arrived at it, that you are truly in the work and in the place God would have you be. The old adage 'Do not go into the ministry if you can do anything else' seems to be out of fashion today. More emphasis is put on encouraging young men who seem appropriately gifted to enter the ministry in some form. There is not necessarily an antithesis between (wise) encouragement from others and being sure of a call of God on your life. What must be understood however is that it is God, not man, who makes a minister. A merely gifted man may make a decent job of it while the sun is shining. When the storm comes, he will also need to be sure that he is there because God wants him to be.

It is not a contradiction of that to say that a minister should be able to say sincerely, 'Lord, if you do not want me here, move me now; even get me out of the ministry; but if you want me here, give me grace and strength to persevere.' When God shows that he wants you where you are, it is a wonderful source of strength.

Paul was also strongly aware that God's judgement, not man's, is what matters (1 Corinthians 4:4-5). He was not cavalier about what people thought of him, but he knew that neither his own nor any other human judgement was ultimate. Only what God thinks is final; assessment of your ministry must therefore be subject to Scripture, and in the end on God's providential ordering of things. If you have to endure the unjust dealings of people, then accept God's will as being what is best for you at this time.

Paul also knew what it was to have a clear conscience (1 Corinthians 4:4). When you are under fire, you need to know first that the issue over which you are fighting is worth it, and secondly that your stance is one over which you have a clear conscience before God. Don't adopt a strong stance on so-called principle, for example, if it may simply be disguised pride or a desire to get your own way. You also need to know that you have handled the matter with integrity. Paul asserted, for example, of his preaching: 'Therefore, having this ministry by the mercy of God, we do not lose heart. But we have renounced disgraceful, underhanded ways. We refuse to practise cunning or to tamper with God's word, but by the open statement of the truth we would commend ourselves to everyone's conscience in the sight of God' (2 Corinthians 4:1–2).

Under pressure you may make mistakes, but making an honest apology over one mistake is not the end of the world and should not deter you from taking a stand on another, perhaps bigger, issue. A clear conscience is not only a beautiful thing to have before God, it is a source of great strength in any conflict and under criticism on spiritual matters.

Finally, Paul was content with 'insult' (2 Corinthians 12:9–10). Probably many ministers have had to endure insults, although some may be fortunate enough not to. Preaching is always an easy thing for people to have a go at, and few things hurt a preacher more than to be told that his preaching is in some way inadequate. You may be told, publicly as well as privately, that your preaching (which you will admit is very defective in many ways) is too difficult, not applied enough, too long, not Christ-centred, not dynamic; that you are too intellectual, or too simplistic. You may be criticised for being harsh when you are preaching the gospel faithfully, including the 'bad' news of sin, wrath and hell; you may be accused of watering down the gospel by sincere Christians who do not think they are hearing enough of those truths. You may be charged with being too heavy, too light, lacking power or not having enough illustrations. You may even be told that you are not really called to preach.

In terms of character, ability or style you may be called too autocratic; too Baptist (or whatever other denominational label your critic thinks fits); not wise; that a church member (who will normally at such times say 'we' or 'many of us') has no confidence in you. Probably many pastors will have had worse. Many of these one may admit, and more; some you will work on; others, you will conclude, are simply not true.

Constructive criticism is (usually) easier to take—the only obstacle is our pride; but too many critical comments are made to weaken, to wound or at best made carelessly and thoughtlessly. They feel like insults. Can I be content with them? I need to apply Paul's words to myself.

Fundamental to Paul's attitude is the principle that 'We have become, and are still, like the scum of the world, the refuse of all things' (1 Corinthians

4:12). That self-assessment makes you content with insult. Indeed, most insults sound like a compliment after that.

Paul responded to criticism very reasonably. When necessary, he explained a situation that had given rise to criticism, such as his changes of plan with regard to his Corinthian visits (2 Corinthians 1:15–2:4). A lesser man might have got irritated with the Corinthians' carping and their readiness to assume the worst—that Paul was vacillating in his plans, rather than that there may have been a good reason for his changes, indeed that he had their interests at heart. Paul makes his point strongly, but he does actually explain things carefully.

Do not dismiss people just because they criticise or are even hostile. The Lord Jesus adopted a similar approach with the Sadducees and other leaders; even maliciously motivated questions often got a straight answer. Sometimes you answer a fool according to his folly; and sometimes you don't. You have to know the fool.

In Corinth he taught and strove for the basic problem of worldly attitudes to be undermined— divisiveness, pride in gifts, lovelessness, misunderstanding about gifts and the body, unbelief in the bodily resurrection, etc. He doesn't just attack the surface problems but his whole discussion of the varied issues at Corinth is informed by determination to correct the basic worldliness and pride of the Corinthians. In Galatia he taught clearly on any particular truth that was being opposed—the doctrine of justification by faith alone. Be prepared to tackle head on any subversion of the gospel.

You should ask—what is behind this attack on me, this criticism? Do you see a common thread which is revealing something wrong in the spiritual life of the church?

Integral to his response to criticism was the life Paul lived. He modelled the cross-centred life. He suffered for the faith and for the faithful (2 Corinthians 4:7-18; 11:16-12:10; Galatians 6:17—he bore in his body the 'marks of Jesus'; cf Colossians 1:24). He did not claim his rights (1 Corinthians 9:12-18). He gave to the churches founded through him not only his preaching but himself (1 Thessalonians 2:1-12). The public ministry and the life of the minister must be at one, or there will be no credible answers to criticism. Your people will struggle to listen to you preaching on loving one another, for example, if they regularly experience harshness from or outside the pulpit. He was patient, as he advised Timothy to be: 'And the Lord's servant must not be quarrelsome but kind to everyone, able to teach, patiently enduring evil, correcting his opponents with gentleness. God may perhaps grant them

repentance leading to a knowledge of the truth ...'
(2 Timothy 2:24–25).

Summary

The first and most basic principle is to expect criticism. When we see the lives of our Lord and of Paul it is amazing that we are receiving, if we are doing our job, as little criticism as we are.

The second is, do not let this criticism stop you. Learn from it, change where need be but keep on doing good—that is, persevere in your ministry; and particularly keep on preaching—and do not let opposition in any form silence the proclamation of the word of God. That, above all, would give Satan delight.

What else can we do when we are criticised? In following the examples of Christ and Paul, what practical steps can we take? After all, there is a crucial difference between what they faced and what we do: criticism of and opposition to our Lord was never justified, and in the context of his infallible apostolic teaching Paul too is writing as one of whom criticism was not justified. Criticism of us will often be justified.

How Should You Respond to Criticism?

Can you give thanks for this criticism?

This may seem a ridiculous question when one considers how hurtful criticism can be. Yet we have seen in 2 Corinthians 12:9-10 that Paul gloried in, among other things, insults, or 'acts of insolence' knowing that this was in God's purposes to enable him to experience more of the sufficiency of God's grace. Hard though it may be to grasp now, all things do work together for good for those who are called according to his purpose (Romans 8:28). In an address on coping with criticism (given at Whiteabbey in Northern Ireland) Joel Beeke quotes John 13:7: 'what I am doing you do not understand now, but afterward you will understand.' This is a promise to us in all kinds of affliction.

Thankfulness is a Christian duty at all times. Three times in a few short sentences the apostle exhorts the Colossians to be thankful (Colossians 3:12-17). Ingratitude is a first symptom of idolatry (Romans 1:21). We need to be careful here. Paul would never have given thanks that the Corinthians were proud, immoral and worldly. Yet he can give thanks for his experience of the personal abuse that he suffered, both physically and verbally. He gave thanks not because there was anything good in what was happening in Corinth or in what he suffered in itself, but because he saw the good hand of God behind it and in it *for him.* It was part of his bearing the cross, of sharing Christ's sufferings, leading to knowing Christ better.

Bearing criticism can therefore be a way in which the minister is drawn closer to Christ. A church member once said to me, only half-jokingly, 'I shall be your thorn in the flesh'. I thought it was a strange thing for a Christian to say. But then, looking at 2 Corinthians 12:9–10, who gets the blessing? Give thanks! Remember that your critic may, in God's providence, be saying something your friends should be saying but do not dare. Your enemy may be your best friend.

Thankfulness gets things in perspective: it reminds us of the sovereignty of God and his goodness. It will cause you to remember all his gifts and benefits to you in Jesus Christ. You remember as the early Christians did that he is the Ruler of all things and all people, including your enemies (Acts 4:23–28).

Understand, if possible, what people are thinking, not just what they say

There is a danger of over-sensitivity to and pre-occupation with *what you hear.* The real issue is not necessarily the words but what lies behind the them. Don't content yourself with guessing, be bold. Ask people to be clear as to what they mean if there is some criticism that is either unclear to you, or veiled by the speaker due to muddle in their own minds, to cowardice or to timidity. If you are not clear, the likelihood is that your imagination will go into overdrive and you will get things out of proportion. Sometimes people's comments are considered, sometimes they are said in an angry moment or as a throw-away remark. Learn to distinguish these.

Be careful too about allowing your imagination to be a slave to what you overhear; a comment about the sermon you overhear on a Sunday evening can ruin your night's sleep, your assessment of the day, and most of your Monday. As for anonymous criticisms—cowardly little letters and notes—some ministers, with justification, advise that you ignore them. Perhaps an alternative approach might help: ignore the issue of source and motive but evaluate the content. Even these may have something to teach you.

It is important not to take everything that comes over as a criticism too seriously or at face value. Some things you can safely ignore; sometimes it could just be your being too thin-skinned; at other times you need to get to what lies behind the words.

Look for the truth in it

Criticism will often be justified. We have to be able to distinguish therefore between what is justified and what is not and respond accordingly.

The first thing is to look for the element of truth in a criticism. Examine your own eye for beams before accusing your critic of having what, after all, may be only a speck. Be approachable, open to reason—one of the qualities of godly wisdom (James 3:17). There are some things to consider that may help.

- Don't respond at once if you can help it.

- Don't respond to email criticism by email—they are too quick to write, too easy to send. Even if you compose a careful email response—leave it overnight. Read and reread your email and consider carefully how it might be interpreted. Talk to someone else about it if possible.

- Think, pray, examine your heart.

- Consider Scripture -remember to entrust yourself to him who judges justly (1 Peter 2:23) as Jesus did.

- Tell yourself that any criticism of you can never be as bad as you really deserve, and be thankful that your critic does not know as much about you as God knows. In other words, get off your high horse and be humble. Be glad that people do not know what you really are.

- Speak to a fellow elder or church leader, or a trusted friend if it is more personal than church related, or your wife (not automatically—your wife is not necessarily to be burdened with your church leadership problems nor are other people's confidences to be shared with her).

- If the criticism is fair, admit that, thank the person and act on it, maybe apologizing, confessing a sin or correcting an action or reversing a decision, as appropriate.

- If it is partly fair and partly unfair, deal with it appropriately. Admit the fair bit, not backing down on the rest.

- If it is fair but harshly, ungraciously or even maliciously expressed, respond graciously, admitting the truth of the substance but also pointing out the wrong mode of expression. If the criticism has been made in public, for example in a church meeting, it may be that a public apology for the manner of expression is called for but it may be better for the church to see you turning the other cheek.

My personal experience has been that very few criticisms have no grain of truth in them. I can learn from them in some way. At the very least it makes me examine my own heart and see the depth of pollution there that needs to be dealt with, even if this criticism is not particularly fair in itself.

If you are of the opinion that there is no or very little truth in the criticism, then remember the Lord Jesus 'who endured such hostility from sinners against himself so that you will not grow weary or fainthearted' (Hebrews 12:3).

Consider the source and the circumstances

I put this after the consideration of the substance because if you consider the person and circumstances first, you can prejudice your ability to listen objectively to the criticism. You may be tempted to say automatically of some people 'well, he would say that wouldn't he?'

Nonetheless it is important to consider the source and circumstances of the criticism:

- Is it a case of 'the grass is always greener ...'—a condition of permanent discontent that afflicts some church members?

- Is the critic someone for whom nothing you say or do will ever be right? Take that into account but don't thereby just ignore the criticism. They may still be right.

- Is it someone who has a long-standing tussle with all authority?

- Is it from someone who is ill, or has a big worry

in his life—illness in the family, unemployment, anxieties about children or parents?

- Sometimes an incident in church may have uncovered or revived an old scar—a slight in the past. 'When I wanted to do this 10 years ago the deacons dismissed it. Now they are spending £20,000 on it.'

- Is it from someone who cannot accept you as pastor, for whatever reason? It can be particularly difficult to follow a long and successful pastorate or a much-loved pastor.

- Is this a bad time to be changing things? People can take so much change, but maybe this is one step too far at this time and you get an explosion.

- Is change necessary and you are obstructing a necessary step forward for the church?

- Think about the reality of the situation, not just what you hear. It may be the tip of an iceberg in the church; or it may be an unrepresentative bit of malice. Don't be cowed by that favourite line of grumblers 'People are saying ...' or 'I know a lot of people who ...'

- Is it from someone who is a true friend whose comments and opinion you value? Then listen carefully, but even then, weigh it up. Your friend may not be right all the time!

There are many things to take into consideration. Be wise; pray for wisdom (James 1:5).

Be more concerned for God's glory and the welfare of the church than for your feelings

You are the under-shepherd. God has placed you in the flock to care for it and you are to give your life for the flock. Will you not put up with criticism for them? It is their welfare that counts in the end, not your own. Think too of your encouragements (though I know that sometimes these can seem few!). Make your highest concern the glory of God and then the good of his people. Moses was prepared to die, even to lose his salvation, rather than see God wipe out the people and the Lord's promises be seen to be unfulfilled (Exodus 32:31–32; cf Numbers 14:11–16; and remember Paul's love for Israel, Romans 9:3).

Be more concerned about what God thinks of you than what people think

Preoccupation with human criticism can distract attention from what God thinks of you, from the standards he sets and from self-examination in the light of his word. We should be assessing ourselves in the light of God's word anyway; over-anxiety about criticism can suggest that we are more subject to the fear of man than the fear of God. Remember Paul's view of human judgement in 1 Corinthians 4:1–5:

This is how one should regard us, as servants of Christ and stewards of the mysteries of God. Moreover, it is required of stewards that they be found faithful. But with me it is a very small thing that I should be judged by you or by any human court. In fact, I do not even judge myself. For I am not aware of anything against myself, but I am not thereby acquitted. It is the Lord who judges me. Therefore do not pronounce judgment before the time, before the Lord comes, who will bring to light the things now hidden in darkness and will disclose the purposes of the heart. Then each one will receive his commendation from God.

Remember basic spirituality

Like thankfulness, the basic spiritual duties of the Christian life do not stop applying to you because you are a pastor or because you are facing opposition. Read the grace-filled imperatives of Romans 12:9–21:

Let love be genuine. Abhor what is evil; hold fast to what is good. Love one another with brotherly affection. Outdo one another in showing honour. Do not be slothful in zeal, be fervent in spirit, serve the Lord. Rejoice in hope, be patient in tribulation, be constant in prayer. Contribute to the needs of the saints and seek to show hospitality.

Bless those who persecute you; bless and do not curse them. Rejoice with those who rejoice, weep with those who weep. Live in harmony with one another. Do not be haughty, but associate with the lowly. Never be wise in your own sight. Repay no one evil for evil, but give thought to do what is honourable in the sight of all. If possible, so far as it depends on you, live peaceably with all. Beloved, never avenge yourselves, but leave it to the wrath of God, for it is written, "Vengeance is mine, I will repay, says the Lord." To the contrary, "if your enemy is hungry, feed him; if he is thirsty, give him something to drink; for by so doing you will heap burning coals on his head." Do not be overcome by evil, but overcome evil with good.

Or Colossians 3:12–17

Put on then, as God's chosen ones, holy and beloved, compassionate hearts, kindness, humility, meekness, and patience, bearing with one another and, if one has a complaint against another, forgiving each other; as the Lord has forgiven you, so you also must forgive. And above all these put on love, which binds everything together in perfect harmony. And let the peace of Christ rule in your hearts, to which indeed you were called in one body. And be thankful. Let the word of Christ dwell in you richly, teaching and admonishing one another in all wisdom, singing psalms and hymns and spiritual songs, with thankfulness in your hearts to God. And whatever you do, in word or deed, do everything in the name of the Lord Jesus, giving thanks to God the Father through him.

Helpful too are Psalms 7 and 13; 1 Timothy 6:11–16; 2 Timothy 2; 1 Peter 2:18–25.

Psalm 13 ends:

But I have trusted in your steadfast love;
my heart shall rejoice in your salvation.
I will sing to the LORD,
because he has dealt bountifully with me. (vv.5–6)

Work hard at forgiveness and reconciliation

Remember to forgive, and do not let bitterness poison your thoughts. Some treatment at the hands of others can leave deep scars—and that includes what church members sometimes receive from pastors. Whatever the situation, forgive each other, as the Lord has forgiven you (Colossians 3:13). This takes time; true forgiveness is not usually the work of a moment; it has to be worked at and repeated in your mind. Reconciliation, the restoration of a relationship when there has been repentance so that forgiveness has been received, may not be possible if there is no repentance (Luke 17:3–4). However at least cultivate the disposition to forgive, the willingness gladly to forgive were the other party to repent. Remember the cross and think of what the Lord has forgiven you.

Critics do sometimes repent. A friend recalled

how two or three years after a bitter experience, he had a phone call from one of those involved, saying how he regretted his part in what had gone on and wished he could undo the past. It seemed to be a genuine attempt at apology and even repentance. That doesn't always happen; many men live without hearing any expressions of regret from their critics, much less repentance. The Lord will judge—we leave it in his hands.

Care for your family

Your wife will be very hurt by what you suffer. It is sometimes easier for the minister to forgive than it is for her. He can often do something about it; she so often has to suffer in silence. Remember what your wife goes through when you are under attack: talk, pray, comfort, help, understand.

Your children will almost certainly pick up what is going on, however hard you try to be discreet. Protect them as much as possible from bitterness against individuals and against the church. You must lead in this, setting an example of Christ-like love.

Pressing on

The most important thing you can do is persevere in all godliness. Don't let the issue get you down or stop you preaching and practicing the truth. Remember that too much absorption with criticism is a sign of pride, perhaps forgetting that you are called to a life of conflict. The disciple after all is not above his master.

Even when there is no truth in a criticism you can benefit from the heart-searching it should cause you. There is always something you need to adjust or put right in your ministry. However do not allow criticism to deflect you from your rightful path.

It is important therefore to have clear goals in ministry, or you can easily be derailed.

- know that you are called, as Paul did;

- know what your authority is, as Christ and the apostles did;

- know what you believe, even on 'secondary' issues. Things that previous generations might have considered sacrosanct or unquestionable are today up for grabs. It is an exciting time to be a pastor but also a stressful and demanding time. This is not just on major issues in society like the meaning of marriage, our attitude to homosexuality and gender issues, but on forms of worship, modes of communicating the gospel and structures of church life. Difficult though it is, a minister must know what he believes on things which a couple of generations ago he might not even have had to think about. We cannot dodge the issues by treating 'secondary' as if it meant 'unimportant'. Secondary things can be very important. So know where you want to go, what you intend to hold fast, and where you are prepared to be flexible. Whatever you do you will be criticised by somebody—but you can ensure that as little as possible is justified!

- create an environment in the church where people feel they can comment, ask questions, suggest improvements and discuss how things are going without being made to feel that they are criticising. Do not be touchy or give your members the impression that you are. Be 'open to reason' (James 3:17). If people do not feel free to approach you or other leaders without being made to feel that their every opinion is unwelcome, unimportant or a threat, it will create hidden but real frustrations that will emerge unpleasantly at some point.

- know where you want to lead the church. Taking criticism constructively can help; criticism can be a hindrance if we let it deflect us or cause us to be so despondent that it reduces our usefulness.

- apply the Reformation principle *semper reformanda* (always reforming) to your own assumptions, particularly on issues where the great creeds and confessions are silent. Sometimes we carry into ministry second-hand opinions or opinions formed on the basis of cursory exegesis. Our congregations are more likely to follow the example of the Bereans if they see us, first, testing everything by Scripture.

What kept me going in the darkest times was my confidence that the Lamb was on the throne, that I examined my heart before God and never had a serious doubt that I was called into the ministry—I was very glad then that I had taken time about entering it and waited until 'I could do nothing else.' A clear conscience, and the conviction that whatever mistakes I had made along the way my fundamental theological and biblical position was right, and the help and encouragement of God's people, inside and outside the church—these have been invaluable

When one church voted a minister out, within a few days he had preaching engagements in evangelical churches for several weeks in his diary. God was good in encouraging him through his people; the Lord was telling him he still had a ministry.

Consider eternity

Joel Beeke concludes his Whiteabbey address on this subject with a reminder to covet the Lord's 'Well done, thou good and faithful servant' (Matthew 25:21).

You will receive the unfading crown of glory when the chief shepherd appears (1 Peter 5:4). You will see that it has all been for your good, both the justified and unjustified criticism; that you have been far worse than your critics ever thought you were but that you have received more grace than could be thought possible; that your ministry has after all been only by God's mercy, and the fact that you have been enabled to continue in it at all is a source of wonder to the angels and should be to you, and one day will be. Criticism, however harsh, unjustified and hurtful will be seen to have been part of that 'slight momentary affliction' that is preparing for you an eternal weight of glory beyond all comparison (2 Corinthians 4:17).

So endure, press on towards the goal, for the prize of the upward call of God in Christ Jesus (Philippians 3:14).

Appendix

Here is part of a letter one minister received from a friend (a retired nurse) in the aftermath of a difficult time:

In this respect my own experience is that of wondering how I could have made such a bad mistake in trusting them which of course is nothing other than PRIDE.

May I use the analogy of a physical wound healing to that of the process of spiritual/psychological/emotional healing? Any wound, but especially a deep one, *must* heal from its base upwards, otherwise there is trouble. If healing takes place from the sides, a channel called a sinus is left, often trapping material eg blood, pus, which causes real problems. Also, a sinus is difficult to eradicate.

To prevent this occurring, a drainage tube is inserted to allow harmful material to evacuate and also to prevent healing from the sides of the wound to occur. As drainage diminishes, so the tube is gradually withdrawn and shortened, indicating that healing from the bottom of the wound is taking place. The tube is removed when drainage ceases and normal healing can then proceed—upwards and not sideways.

Another aspect of wound healing is that of not trying to hurry the procedure otherwise an excess of tissue can form over the wound site (called proud! flesh) which has to be cauterized. This can cause scar tissue problems.

Transferring all this to the spiritual/psychological realm must mean that when we have been deeply wounded, that which has been most affected has to be thoroughly dealt with, if healthy healing is to take place.

What I find the most difficult thing to deal with is SELF, often in the form of hurt pride leading to anger.

Anger is a natural reaction to pain. But we have to honestly consider to whom the anger is directed: those who have caused the hurt; ourselves, for trusting them; God, for allowing such a situation to develop, especially when what we were trying to do was His will and for his honour. Maybe our anger incorporates all of these.

Bitterness is tied up with anger, and so is revenge. We need to remember Romans 12:19, 'Beloved, do not avenge yourselves, but rather give place to wrath; for it is written, "Vengeance is mine, I will repay, says the Lord"'. He does, and in his way and time and sometimes it is a long time before he acts, but that is his prerogative. We have to learn to patiently trust his wise judgements.

Exodus 15:22–25 is a passage which directs us where to go in our painful situations and struggles. Moses 'cried out to the Lord and the Lord showed him a tree; and when he cast it into the waters, the waters were made sweet. There he made a statute and an ordinance for them. And there he tested them'. We all know what the tree means. Nothing less than the power of Calvary can turn our bitter waters into sweet waters. As Amy Carmichael writes,

'So blessed Lord, in all our Marah days,
Show us the tree; one thought of Calvary's cross
Makes bitter sweet, discovers gain in loss.
Let not your heart be troubled Thou didst say
Long, long ago. It is Thy word today'.

(From *Edges of His Ways*)

Whenever the unwelcome thoughts present themselves, it is paramount that we fly to the cross—for cleansing and for the strength and grace to die to self, lay everything before the Lord, and then deliberately turn one's mind to something totally different and concentrate on that. And it need not be something of a spiritual nature. It is very therapeutic.

There is the old enemy too, to recognize, who loves to disturb our peace and trouble our conscience like the man with the muck-rake in *Pilgrim's Progress*, keeping us from looking at the

Lord, by concentrating on that which is of the flesh. The cross is the answer to this.

The Lord responds to our honest and earnest desire to deal with wounds and leads us on at the pace we are able and willing to go. He knows what we can cope with at any given time, and he never violates personality, temperament, natural or even regional characteristics, nor hang-overs from heredity and upbringing. All of these play a part in our reaction to whatever befalls us, and we ignore this to our detriment. The Lord always leads and never drives, or he draws. Our part is to respond positively to him and his tender loving dealings with us.

Dear brother, the Lord will bring you through this trial with profit to your own life and those to whom you minister. He will do this in a way best suited to you personally.